W9-BHG-505

SWING

By S.L. Hamilton

VISIT US AT ABDOPUBLISHING.COM

Published by ABDO Publishing Company, 8000 West 78th Street, Suite 310, Edina, MN 55439. Copyright ©2011 by Abdo Consulting Group, Inc. International copyrights reserved in all countries. No part of this book may be reproduced in any form without written permission from the publisher. A&D Xtreme™ is a trademark and logo of ABDO Publishing Company.

Printed in the United States of America, North Mankato, Minnesota.
112010
012011

 PRINTED ON RECYCLED PAPER

Editor: John Hamilton
Graphic Design: Sue Hamilton
Cover Design: John Hamilton
Cover Photo: Corbis
Interior Photos: AP-pgs 4, 5, 9, 15, 19 & 23; Corbis-pgs 1, 13, 17, 18, 22, 28, 30 & 31; Getty Images-pgs 6, 7, 8, 10, 14, 16, 26, 29 & 32; Adam Larkey/ABC via Getty-Pg 20 bottom image; Kelsey McNeal/ABC via Getty-pgs 10 & 11, pg 20 top image, pg 21, & pg 25; iStock-pgs 24 (loafers) & 26; New York Times-pg 8; Orange County Archives-pg 12; Shorty George Snowden-pg 8; ThinkStock-pgs 2, 3, 24 (Oxfords, Mary Janes, tennis shoes).

Library of Congress Cataloging-in-Publication Data

Hamilton, Sue L., 1959-
  Swing / S.L. Hamilton.
    p. cm. -- (Xtreme dance)
  ISBN 978-1-61714-734-0
  1. Swing (Dance) I. Title.
  GV1796.S85H36 2011
  793.3'3--dc22
                      2010037643

CONTENTS

XTREME

Swing dancers mix tap dancing, jazz steps, and acrobatics to create a wild, fast dance routine.

SWING

"We're fools whether we dance or not, so we might as well dance." ~Japanese Proverb

SWING

Swing dancing began among African Americans in the 1920s in New York City. Harlem's Savoy Ballroom, which opened in 1926, played jazz music. People of all races flocked to swing dance on its block-long dance floor.

Xtreme Fact

Famous dancers Willa Mae Ricker and Leon James invented many swing steps at the Savoy.

HISTORY

DANCE

Lindy Hop

A union of the 1920s Breakaway and Charleston dances, the Lindy Hop is credited to dancer "Shorty" George Snowden. He named it after pilot Charles Lindbergh's first solo flight from New York to Paris in 1927. The flight was called a "hop" across the Atlantic Ocean.

The New York Times.

THE WEATHER

"All the News That's Fit to Print."

NEW YORK, SUNDAY, MAY 22, 1927.

LINDBERGH DOES IT! TO PARIS IN 33½ HOURS; FLIES 1,000 MILES THROUGH SNOW AND SLEET; CHEERING FRENCH CARRY HIM OFF FIELD

COULD HAVE GONE 500 MILES FARTHER

Gasoline for at Least That Much More—Flew at Times From 10 Feet to 10,000 Feet Above Water.

ATE ONLY ONE AND A HALF OF HIS SANDWICHES

Fell Asleep at Times but Quickly Awoke—Glimpse of His Adventures in Brief Interview at the Embassy.

CROWD ROARS THUNDEROUS WELCOME

Breaks Through Lines of Soldiers and Police and Surging to Plane Lifts Weary Flier from His Cockpit

AVIATORS SAVE HIM FROM FRENZIED MOB OF 100,000

Paris Boulevards Ring With Celebration After Day and Night Watch—American Flag Is Called For and Wildly Acclaimed.

LINDBERGH TRIUMPH THRILLS COOLIDGE

LEVINE ABANDONS BELLANCA FLIGHT

PASSENGERS ON SHIPS HAIL LINDBERGH HOP

Snowden

STYLES

STYLES

Xtreme Quote "The Lindy Hop... We flying just like Lindy did!" ~George Snowden

Jitterbug

The Jitterbug name came from a term used in the 1920s for alcoholics with the shakes or the "jitters." Popular singer and band leader Cab Calloway made the dance famous with his 1934 tune "Jitterbug." In the 1950s, the dance style changed and was performed to rock and roll music.

Cab Calloway

They look like a bunch of jitterbugs out there on the floor.

Balboa

In the 1930s, dancers at the Balboa Pavilion in Newport Beach, California, created their own swing dance style. Because the older club's small building couldn't withstand the wild acrobatics of the Jitterbug, dancers created the Balboa. This dance uses fast footwork, but no wild tosses or breakaways. It worked well on the small dance floor.

Balboa Pavilion

Balboa Dancers

The Balboa is also known as "Pure Bal."
Dancers stay in close contact
with each other, moving as a couple.

West Coast Swing

Developed by dancer Dean Collins in the 1930s and 1940s, West Coast Swing was often used in Hollywood movies of the era. It uses more turns and footwork, along with more hand and arm motion.

Dean Collins

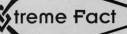

Xtreme Fact The West Coast Swing is the official state dance of California.

Dancers Heidi Groskreutz and Benji Schwimmer are West Coast Swing champions.

Shag and Whip

Shag was created in Texas, North Carolina, South Carolina, and Missouri. Shaggers do basic six-count hopping steps, mostly facing their partners. Whip is a swing dance performed to slower rhythm-and-blues tunes. It was developed in Texas and features spinning moves.

Dancing the Shag.

Whip was first known as the
Cat Dance, because all the
"cool cats" were dancing the Whip.

East Coast Swing

The East Coast Swing grew from the moves of the Lindy Hop and the Jitterbug in New York. It is a quick step with many wraps, tunnels, and turns. A wrap is an inside underarm turn. A tunnel takes the partner under and around the body.

XTREME

Swing dancers perform floor steps and aerials, or air steps. These are high-energy, acrobatic moves. Partners must be careful to be in the right place at the right time to avoid injury.

MOVES

SWING

Loose, comfortable clothing defines the swing dancer's style. Women often wear wide circle skirts. Men are seen in baggy pants and cotton shirts. Big, loose "zoot suits" were first worn in the 1930s and 1940s. They are still worn to dance in today.

Xtreme Definition

Zooty /adj/ Dressed in a zoot suit or in extreme clothing.

FASHION

Hair and Shoe Styles

Since swing dancers move fast, women and men often wear their hair short. Women may also tie up their hair. This keeps hair from blocking their view or hitting their partner. Shoe styles are usually Oxfords or loafers for men. Women often wear low-heeled footwear such as tennis shoes or Mary Janes.

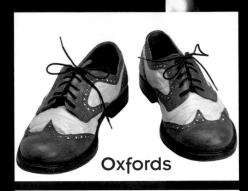
Oxfords

Loafers

Mary Janes

Tennis Shoes

LEARN

Swing dance styles are popular classes at dance studios or exercise clubs. Video lessons are also available on the Internet and on DVDs.

 **Xtreme Fact**

In the early years of swing, talented African American dancers were well paid to give dance lessons to white couples.

TO SWING

DANCE

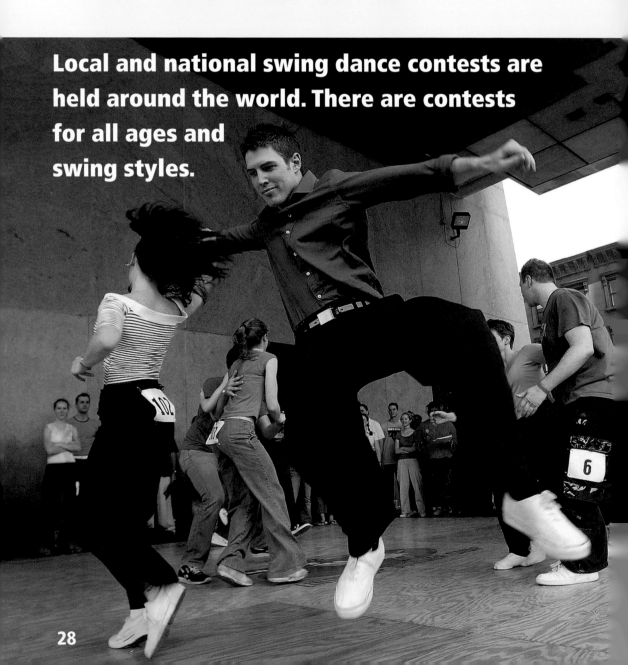

Local and national swing dance contests are held around the world. There are contests for all ages and swing styles.

CONTESTS

The Colors of the Rainbow Team Match is a dance contest for young people.

INDIGO

THE

Aerials / Air Steps

A dance move where one or both of the partners' feet leaves the floor. Swing dancers, especially those doing the Lindy Hop and West Coast Swing, perform such aerial moves as flips, kicks, and jumps.

Breakaway

A dance style from the 1920s. Partners danced together for the most part, then broke away from each other to tap dance independently. Breakaway is considered one of the beginning swing dances.

Charleston

A dance style from the 1920s named for Charleston, South Carolina. The dance was made for solo, group, or partner dancing. "The Charleston," a song by James Johnson, came out in 1923. It popularized the dance. The dance's steps were used to help create the Lindy Hop.

Floor Steps

Dance steps where the feet remain on the floor.

GLOSSARY

Loafers

A low-heeled, comfortable, slip-on shoe.

Mary Janes

A low-heeled shoe with a rounded toe. A strap across the top holds the shoe in place.

Oxfords

A stylish, lace-up shoe with a low heel. Usually considered a man's shoe.

Tunnel

A dance step that brings one of the partners under the arms of another partner.

Wrap

A dance step where partners hold both hands, then move into an inside underarm turn.

Zoot Suit

A suit with a long, oversized jacket and loose pants that taper to tight cuffs at the ankle.

INDEX